THE EARTH

BY HOLLY DUHIG

©2018
Book Life
King's Lynn
Norfolk PE30 4LS

ISBN: 978-1-78637-220-8

Written by:
Holly Duhig
Edited by:
Kirsty Holmes
Designed by:
Danielle Rippengill

A catalogue record for this book
is available from the British Library

PHOTO CREDITS

Abbreviations: l-left, r-right, b-bottom, t-top, c-centre, m-middle.

Front cover – Triff. Back Cover – pixelparticle. 2 – nienora. 4 – sdecoret. 6 – Mopic. 7 – Detelina Petkova. 8 – Jagoush. 9 – Diego Barucco. 10 – Vladi333. 11 – Aphelleon. 12 – Vadim Sadovski. 13 – Vadim Sadovski. 14 – Nadalina. 19t – Mariusz Niedzwiedzki, 19b – Ammit Jack. 20 – Mike Focus. 21 – Natthawon Chaosakun. 22 – solarseven. 23 – Marc Ward. 24 – solarseven. 25t – Jamen Percy, 25b – Reggie Lavoie. 26 – Kletr. 27 – Thaiview. 28 – oorka. 29 – diversepixel. 30t – sdecoret, 30m – 4Max, 30t – sdecoret.

Images are courtesy of Shutterstock.com. With thanks to Getty Images, Thinkstock Photo and iStockphoto.

CONTENTS

PAGE 4   What Is the Earth?

PAGE 6   How Did Earth Get Here?

PAGE 8   Early Earth

PAGE 10   A Home for Life

PAGE 12   The Earth and Other Planets

PAGE 14   Earth and the Moon

PAGE 16   Layers of the Earth

PAGE 18   Plate Tectonics

PAGE 20   Earthquakes

PAGE 22   Earth Under Attack

PAGE 24   Space Weather

PAGE 26   Global Warming

PAGE 28   A New Earth

PAGE 30   Quick Quiz

PAGE 31   Glossary

PAGE 32   Index

Words that look like *this* are explained in the glossary on page 31.

WHAT IS THE EARTH?

The Earth is the name of the planet that 7 billion people and 8.7 billion *species* of animal call home. It is a very special planet because, as far as we know, it is the only planet that can support life. It is often called the 'Goldilocks' planet because, just like her porridge, it is not too hot or too cold; it is just right.

FACT FILE

NAME: Earth
PLANET NUMBER: 3
DISTANCE FROM SUN: 150 million kilometres
Diameter: 12,756 kilometres
NUMBER OF MOONS: 1
ONE YEAR = 365 days
ONE DAY = 24 hours

Earth has plenty to offer the people and animals that call it home. It has lots of water and a thick *atmosphere* with lots of oxygen. Oxygen is the gas all living things need to survive.

There are eight planets in the Solar System, all of which *orbit* the Sun. Earth is the third planet from the Sun. It is the fifth largest planet and the largest of the rocky planets. The Earth takes 365 days to make one complete path around the Sun. We call this a year.

Neptune

Uranus

Saturn

Jupiter

Mars

Earth

Venus

Mercury

The Solar System formed 4.6 billion years ago!

HOW DID EARTH GET HERE?

Everything in our Solar System was formed out of a huge cloud of gases and dust in space, called a nebula. Over time, the material in the nebula was pulled together by *gravity*, which caused it to collapse in on itself until it formed a pancake-like disk.

The centre of the disk became extremely hot and dense until it formed the ball of burning gas we now call the Sun. Pieces of rock and dust on the outer edges of the disk began to collide. Eventually, this process made rocks big enough to become planets with their own gravity. This is how all the planets in the Solar System, including Earth, were formed.

HOW DID THE MOON GET THERE?

Although nobody is certain, scientists have a few theories about why planet Earth has a moon. Many scientists think that, at some point in our planet's history, it was struck by a meteorite the size of Mars which sent huge pieces of rock from the Earth flying into outer space. This material would have eventually been pulled together by gravity to form the Moon.

EARLY EARTH

When Earth began to form 4.5 billion years ago, it was little more than a ball of *molten* rock. The surface of Earth would have been made up of streams of lava and been under constant attack from pieces of space rock.

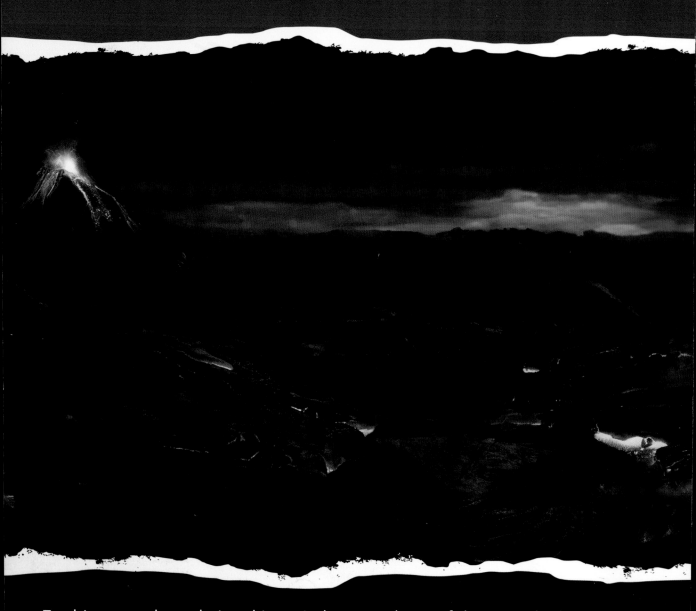

Earth's atmosphere during this period was made up of the gases hydrogen and helium; the same two gases that the Sun is made of. There was no oxygen and because of this, there were no living things.

EARLY ATMOSPHERE

Early Earth was home to lots of violent volcanoes. These erupted and produced lots of new gases that helped make up the atmosphere we have today. Volcanoes also produced water *vapour* which helped form the Earth's oceans.

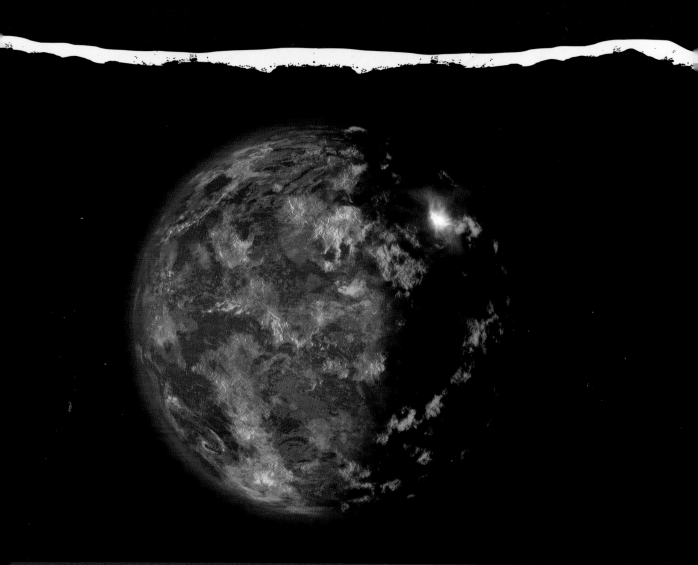

When the Earth was first forming, the Sun wasn't as hot or as bright as it is today. Our planet would have frozen very quickly if it wasn't for volcanoes. Volcanoes release *greenhouse gases* which trap the Sun's heat in the atmosphere and help the planet stay warm.

A HOME FOR LIFE

So, how did the Earth end up becoming the Goldilocks planet?
What made it so perfect for living things?

Water is incredibly important to life and there is plenty of it on Earth. Around 70% of the Earth's surface is covered in water. Most of this water is in the oceans and provides a home for **marine** animals. Only about 2.5% of water on Earth is **freshwater** which land animals, including humans, can drink.

Earth's atmosphere is not too thick or too thin, making it just right to support life. Gases in the atmosphere keep the planet warm by trapping some of the Sun's heat. If our atmosphere was too thick, it would trap too much heat and Earth would become too hot for life to survive.

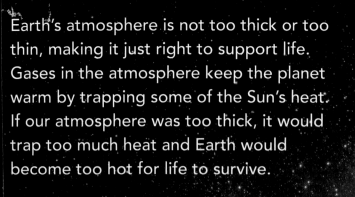

The atmosphere on Venus is 90 times heavier than on Earth. An atmosphere this heavy would crush you!

A thick atmosphere can be very heavy. Atmospheric pressure is the weight of the atmosphere pressing down on us. We don't notice this pressure on Earth because our bodies are used to it but, as you are reading this, 1,000 kilograms of atmospheric pressure is pushing down on you.

THE EARTH AND OTHER PLANETS

The Earth is one of eight planets in the Solar System. It is certainly a very special planet, but how does it compare to its closest neighbours?

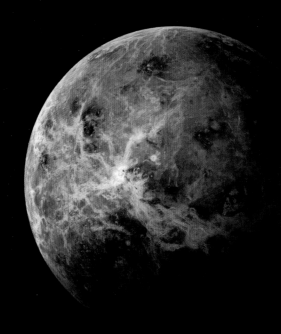

VENUS

Venus is the closest planet to Earth both in distance and size. However, there are some big differences between the two. For example, Venus's atmosphere is so thick that if you were to stand on the planet's surface you would be squashed flat! It would feel the same as being 1,000 kilometres under the ocean on Earth. Venus's atmosphere also contains gases that would be poisonous to humans.

MARS

Mars is the fourth planet from the Sun and, like Earth, it spins on its axis and has seasons. A day on both planets is the same length because both planets take 24 hours to do one full rotation. Both planets also have ice caps at their north and south poles.

Mars has two moons orbiting it called Phobos and Deimos.

However, Mars is much smaller than Earth which means it has weaker gravity. It also has a very thin atmosphere so, if you were to visit Mars, you would need to wear a spacesuit to breathe.

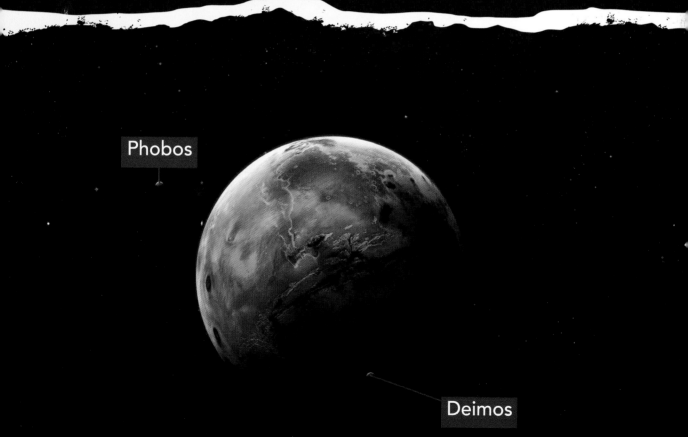

Phobos

Deimos

EARTH AND THE MOON

Many planets in the Solar System, including our own, have moons orbiting them.

The first man to walk on the Moon was Neil Armstrong in 1969.

The Earth has one moon. It orbits Earth every 27 days and it is the only place in the Solar System, besides Earth, that humans have walked on. Despite being 384,400 kilometres away, the Moon affects life on Earth more than we might think.

TIDES

The Moon is responsible for Earth's ocean tides. This is because the Moon's gravity is strong enough to pull the water on Earth towards it. This creates a bulge in the ocean on the side of Earth the Moon is facing. We call this high tide.

There are two high tides and two low tides each day.

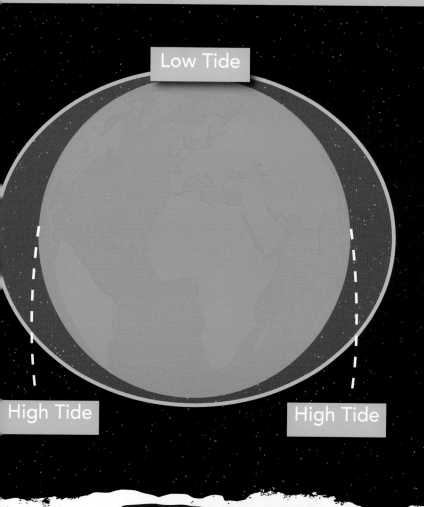

Low Tide

High Tide

High Tide

There will also be a high tide on the side of the Earth facing away from the Moon. This is because the Moon also pulls the whole planet towards it slightly which creates a dip in the seabed on the other side of the planet. Water rushes in to fill this dip creating a high tide.

LAYERS OF THE EARTH

We might think Earth is only made up of the land and water that we can see on its surface, but this is not the case. Earth, like most rocky planets, is made up of many layers. The rocky outer layer of the Earth that we can see is called the crust, and it only makes up 1% of the whole planet.

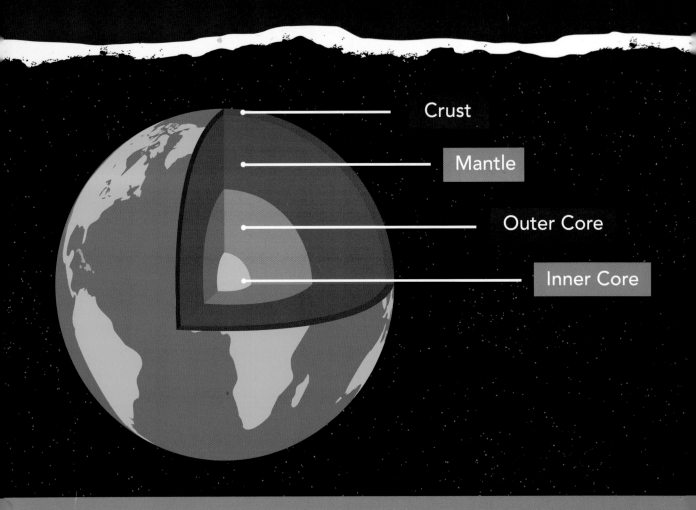

Crust

Mantle

Outer Core

Inner Core

Underneath the crust is the Earth's mantle. This is the thickest layer of the Earth and makes up 84% of the entire planet. It is made up of semi-molten rock called magma, which the Earth's crust sits on.

OUTER CORE

The outer core is a liquid layer deep inside our planet. This liquid is made of melted metals such as iron and nickel. It is about 2,500 kilometres deep in some places.

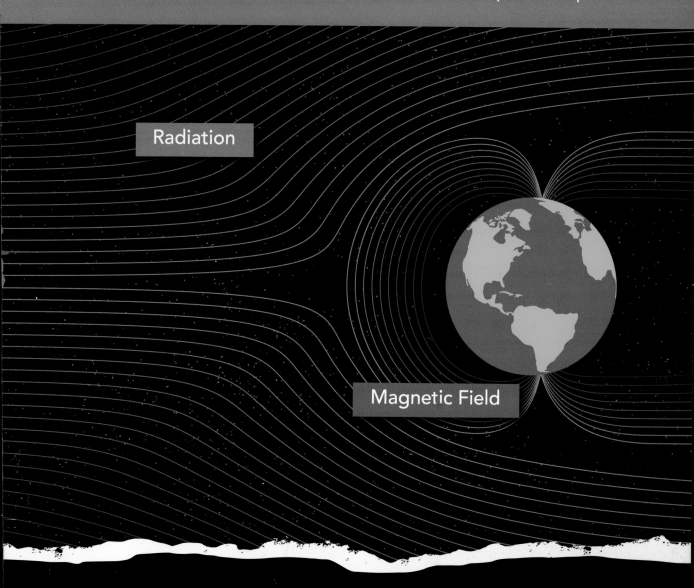

Radiation

Magnetic Field

INNER CORE

Just like the outer core, the inner core is also made of nickel and iron but is solid. This ball of metal is the hottest part of the planet at 6,000°C which is hotter than the surface of the Sun. The metallic outer and inner core are responsible for the Earth's *magnetic field*.

PLATE TECTONICS

The Earth's crust covers all the other layers of the planet but it is not whole. It is broken into large chunks of land called tectonic plates that drift on the Earth's mantle. The movement of tectonic plates is responsible for many of our planet's natural features, such as *continents*, mountains and volcanoes.

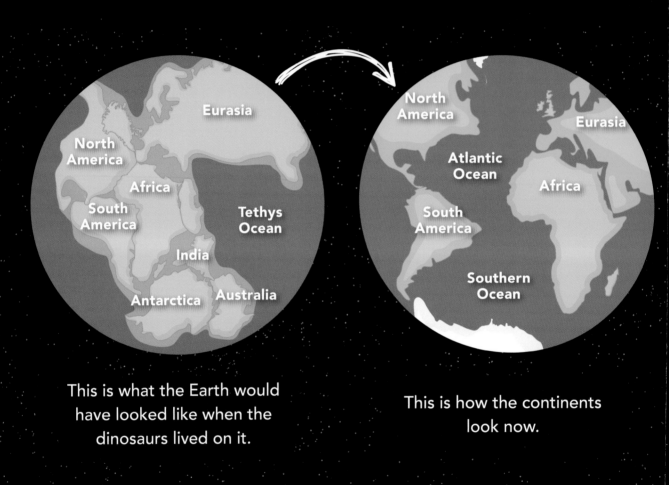

This is what the Earth would have looked like when the dinosaurs lived on it.

This is how the continents look now.

Tectonic plates only move about two to five centimetres each year. This might not seem like very much but, over millions of years, it can make a big difference to the planet's surface. About 250 million years ago, all the continents on Earth were joined together in one giant *landmass* called Pangea.

MOUNTAINS AND VOLCANOES

Mountains and volcanoes are formed by tectonic plates crashing into each other. As tectonic plates push against each other, the Earth's crust is forced upwards. Over thousands of years, this creates rises in the Earth that we call mountains.

Sometimes, this same movement causes magma to rise up through cracks in the Earth's crust. This is how volcanoes form. As the plates continue to push together, pressure is put on the magma which causes it to erupt from the Earth in a powerful explosion.

EARTHQUAKES

Earthquakes are also caused by the movement of tectonic plates. Tectonic plates can collide, pull apart, or slide underneath each other. These movements create cracks in the Earth's crust called fault lines.

The biggest tsunami wave ever recorded was over 520 metres tall.

As tectonic plates move, rocks near the fault lines slip and slide causing earthquakes where the ground shakes violently. Earthquakes that happen under the ocean floor can cause huge ocean waves called tsunamis. Tsunamis can flood towns, cities and coastlines causing destruction and loss of life.

Earthquakes are measured on the Richter scale, which measures how much energy an earthquake produces. They are given a rating. The higher the rating, the stronger the earthquake.

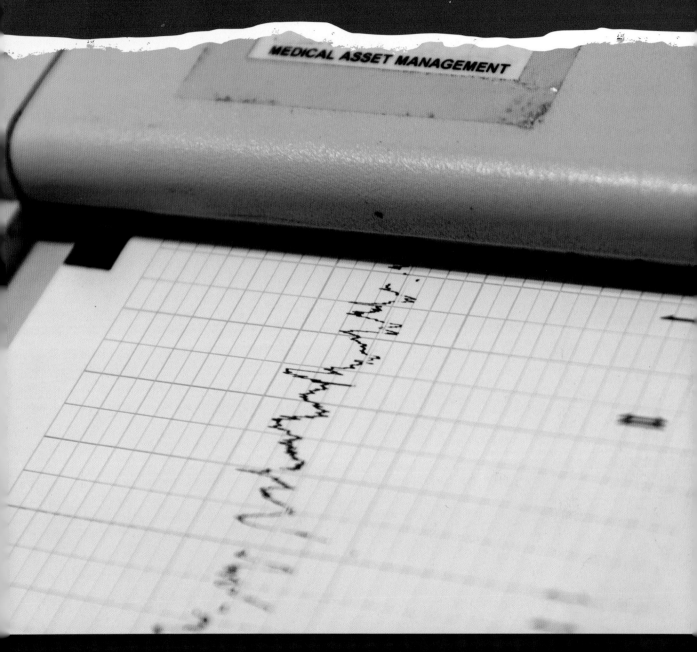

Earthquakes that measure four or below on the Richter scale are counted as mild whereas earthquakes that measure nine or above can destroy whole cities and kill thousands of people. The largest earthquake ever recorded hit Chile on the 22nd of May, 1960. It measured 9.5 on the Richter scale and killed thousands of people.

EARTH UNDER ATTACK

Planet Earth has been bombarded with *meteorites* for billions of years. Meteorites are pieces of space rock that survive falling through the Earth's atmosphere without burning up. Every year, thousands of rocks survive the fall to Earth but we rarely notice them because they are either too small or they land in the sea.

Pieces of rock that do burn up in the Earth's atmosphere are called meteors. Meteors hit the atmosphere at speeds over 40,000 kilometres per hour, which causes the air around them to heat up and destroy the rocks before they can reach the planet's surface.

DEATH OF THE DINOSAURS

If they are big enough, meteorites can cause massive destruction. Some scientists believe it was a meteorite that caused the dinosaurs to go *extinct*. They believe this meteorite would have been ten kilometres wide and landed in shallow sea, near the area we now call Mexico.

This giant piece of space rock would have caused a lot of trouble. It would have started fires, released deadly gases and caused massive earthquakes. Scientists also think it produced a huge dust cloud that blocked out the Sun's light, causing plants to die and many dinosaurs to starve.

SPACE WEATHER

Earth can sometimes be in danger from what we call 'space weather'. Space weather is activity on the surface of the Sun that affects us here on Earth. For example, our Sun will sometimes release huge bursts of energy called solar flares. These explosions leap off the Sun's surface in huge arches that can be up to ten times the size of Earth.

If the full force of energy from a solar flare reached the Earth, we would be in serious danger. Luckily, Earth has a protective shield called the magnetosphere. This is the strong magnetic field that surrounds the Earth thanks to the Earth's metallic core.

You can see how Earth is protected by the magnetosphere on pg.17.

Solar Flare

The magnetic field is weakest at the north and south poles. When energy from a solar flare hits this part of the Earth's magnetosphere, colourful lights called auroras are produced. Auroras that can be seen from northern countries are often called the aurora borealis, and auroras that can be seen from southern countries are called the aurora australis.

A blackout in Quebec, Canada occurred after a coronal mass ejection the size of 36 Earths was propelled from the Sun's surface.

Storms on the surface of the Sun can also produce even bigger explosions called coronal mass ejections. These cause lots of trouble here on Earth. They can damage satellites and even cause power cuts in large areas.

GLOBAL WARMING

Unfortunately for us, space weather isn't the only sort of weather that affects us. Changes in weather patterns here on Earth can also harm our planet.

Since 1880, the Earth's temperature has risen by 0.85°C.

Weather patterns are changing due to a process called global warming. Global warming is the result of humans burning *fossil fuels* such as coal, oil and gas to make electricity. We use electricity to power everything from factories and hospitals to schools and houses. Burning fossil fuels releases greenhouse gases which trap the Sun's heat in the Earth's atmosphere. Overtime, this causes the planet to get hotter.

CARING FOR THE EARTH

Global warming causes flooding in some places and **drought** in others. Such extreme weather patterns harm both humans and animals. But what can we do to help?

1. SAVING ENERGY:

Turning off electrical items when you're not using them saves electricity. The less electricity that is used, the less fossil fuels need to be burned.

2. RENEWABLE ENERGY:

Fossil fuels are non-renewable, meaning they will one day run out. Luckily, we can make electrical energy using wind turbines and solar panels. We call this renewable energy because it comes from things that don't run out such as wind and sunlight.

A NEW EARTH

ALIEN LIFE?

With plenty of oxygen, water and a warm temperature to boot, Earth is the ideal planet to live on. But is it the only place in the universe where living things can thrive? Or is there a possibility of finding life elsewhere?

Our galaxy contains billions of stars and even more planets, so astronomers are always on the lookout for Earth-like planets in other solar systems. But planets are not always easy to find. Astronomers have to search for distant planets by watching out for shadows moving across other stars.

TRAPPIST-1

Astronomers have discovered seven planets orbiting a very small, very dim star called TRAPPIST-1 which is about 39 *light years* away from our own Sun. Although TRAPPIST-1 is not as hot as our Sun, all of its planets orbit it very closely so they don't get too cold. The farthest planet in this solar system is closer to TRAPPIST-1 than Mercury is to our Sun.

Because of this, if you lived on one of these planets, TRAPPIST-1 would look much bigger in the sky than our Sun does but it wouldn't shine as brightly. These seven planets would all be warm enough to have water on their surfaces. This means they are all strong contenders in the race to find alien life. Who knows? Perhaps one day we will be able to pay them a visit!

QUICK QUIZ

How many planets are there in our solar system?

How many times heavier is Venus's atmosphere than Earth's?

How long does it take for Mars to rotate on its axis?

How long does it take for the Moon to orbit the Earth?

What year did the first man walk on the Moon?

What percentage of the Earth is the mantle?

How are mountains formed?

What scale are earthquakes measured on?

What is a solar flare?

What is a space weather?

What causes auroras?

How many planets orbit TRAPPIST-1?

GLOSSARY

ASTRONOMERS	people who study the universe and objects in space
ATMOSPHERE	the mixture of gases that make up the air and surround the Earth
AXIS	the internal point or line around which an object spins, such as a planet or moon
CONTINENTS	very large areas of land on the Earth's surface
DIAMETER	the distance through the centre of an object
EXTINCT	a species of animal that is no longer alive
FOSSIL FUELS	fuels, such as coal, oil and gas, that formed millions of years ago from the remains of animals and plants
FRESHWATER	water that is not salty and doesn't come from the sea
GRAVITY	the force that attracts physical bodies together and increases in strength as a body's mass increases
GREENHOUSE GASES	gases in the atmosphere that trap the Sun's heat
LANDMASS	a large, single body of land
LIGHT YEARS	a measurement based on how far light travels in a year. One lightyear is 9.5 trillion kilometres
MAGNETIC FIELD	a protective force around the world that is created by the liquid and solid cores of the Earth
MARINE	relating to or found in the ocean
METEORITES	pieces of rock that successfully enter a planet's atmosphere without being destroyed
MOLTEN	melted into a liquid using heat
ORBIT	the path that an object makes around a larger object in space
SATELLITES	machines in space that travel around planets, take photographs and collect and transmit information
SPECIES	a group of very similar animals or plants that are capable of producing young together
VAPOUR	a substance in the gaseous state

INDEX

AURORAS 25

ATMOSPHERE 4, 9–13, 22

ATMOSPHERIC PRESSURE 11

AXIS 13

CORE 16–17, 24

CRUST 16, 19–20

DINOSAURS 18, 23

EARTHQUAKES 20–21, 23

GALAXY 28

GLOBAL WARMING 26–27

GOLDILOCKS 4, 10

GRAVITY 6–7, 13, 15

GREENHOUSE GASES 9, 26

JUPITER 5

MAGMA 16, 19

MAGNETIC FIELD 17, 25

MANTLE 16, 18

MARS 5, 7, 13

METEORITES 7, 22–23

MOON 4, 7, 13–15

MOUNTAINS 18–19

NEBULA 6

OCEANS 9–12, 15, 18, 20

ORBIT 5, 13–14, 29

OXYGEN 4, 8, 28

PANGEA 18

TECTONIC PLATES 18–19, 20

TSUNAMIS 20

VENUS 5, 11–12

VOLCANOES 9, 19–19